The Children's First
ATLAS

To Anna, I hope you
Merry x'mas & hope you
enjoy this Book.
Love always from
Auntie Gertrude &
Uncle Alistair.

Author
Brenda Williams

Illustrators
Frederick St. Ward
and Roger Payne

Cartographer
Malcolm Porter

Published in Great Britain by
World International Publishing Limited
P.O. Box 111, Great Ducie Street, Manchester M60 3BL.
Printed in Belgium.
SBN 7235 7055 8.
Reprinted 1985.

Contents

Introduction	8
North and Central America	10
South America	15
Europe	18
The British Isles	22
Africa	24
Asia	28
Australia	38
New Zealand	40
The Pacific Islands	41
The Poles	42
Index	44

Introduction

As the Earth is round, the best kind of 'model' Earth is a globe. But most maps are flat. So the map-maker has to find some way of drawing a curved surface onto flat paper. This is done by using various *projections*. No projection is exactly correct for, though some details of the Earth are shown properly, others are enlarged or distorted in some other way.

Photographs taken from space show our Earth as it really is: a round ball of continents and oceans, wrapped in a thin skin of air, spinning through space.

Modern maps are made with the help of photographs taken from space. Satellites in orbit above the Earth can study the ground below and send back photographs showing the smallest details. The map-maker works from a series of photographs, each one slightly overlapping the one before so that nothing is missed.

Opposite page: A view of the Earth as seen from an Apollo spaceship. Below: Forty-six separate images make up this image of Italy. It does not show Italy as we would see it from space because it is made from an invisible light called infra-red light. Scientists can tell a lot about the land from such pictures. Right: An infra-red picture of the Grand Canyon in the North American Rockies.

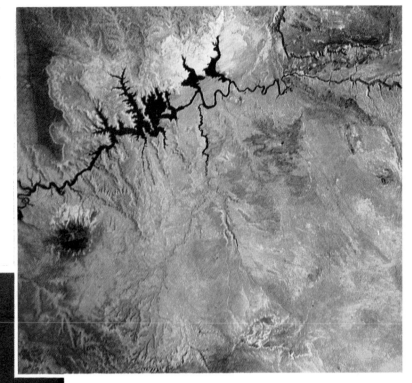

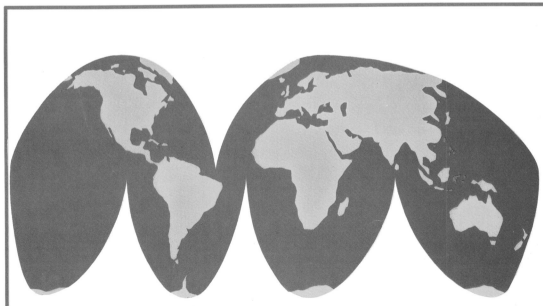

Latitude and Longitude

A map is divided up by lines of latitude (running east to west) and lines of longitude (north to south). A map reference, giving both latitude and longitude, is used to pinpoint the exact position of any place on a map.

The equator is 0 degrees latitude. So the latitude of any place on the Earth is the number of degrees it lies between the equator and the nearest pole (which is at an angle of 90 degrees to the equator). Lines of longitude pass through both the North and South Poles. The line of 0 degrees longitude runs through Greenwich, England, and is known as the Greenwich Meridian. The other lines of longitude run 180 degrees east and west of Greenwich.

It is very difficult to show the curved surface of the Earth as it really is on a flat piece of paper. It is rather like peeling an orange and trying to make the skin lie flat. Some world maps do have this 'peeled-orange' look (left). Maps can be drawn so that one feature, such as the distance between places, is correct. But this means that something else, such as the shape of the land, may be wrong. Maps covering smaller areas, such as part of a country, are more accurate than world maps because there is only a slight curve in the Earth's surface to distort them.

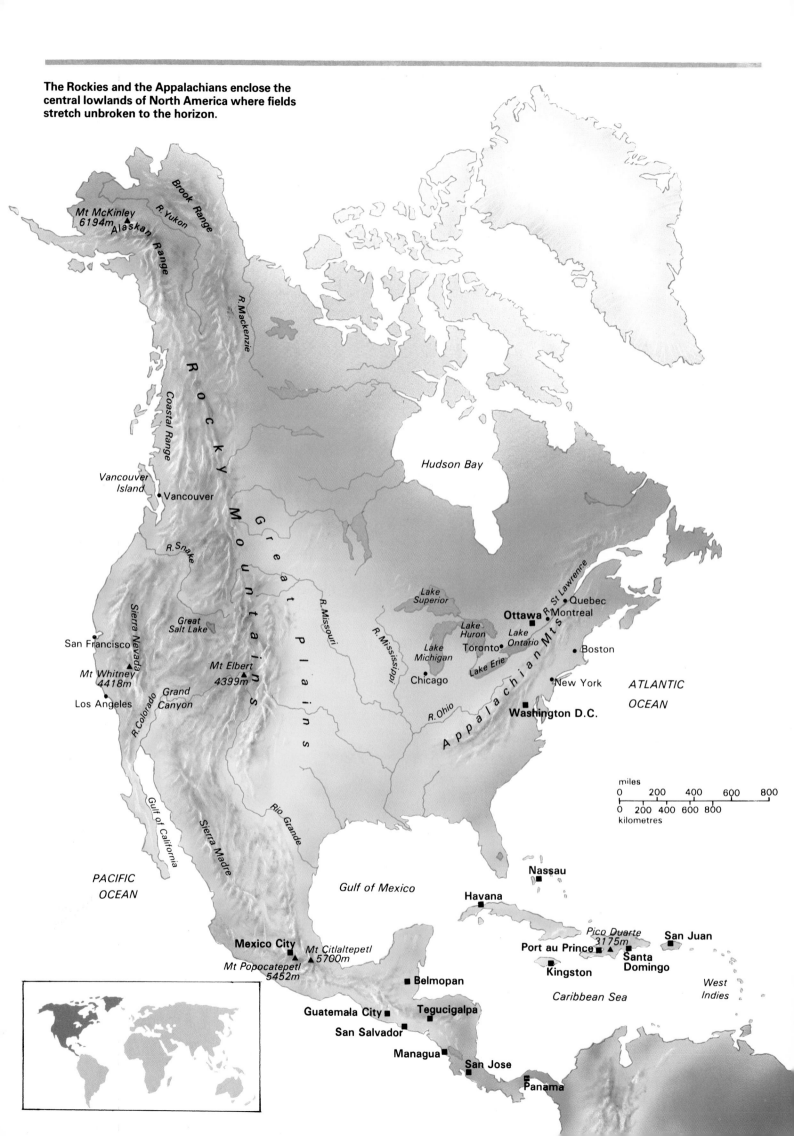

The Rockies and the Appalachians enclose the central lowlands of North America where fields stretch unbroken to the horizon.

Brook Range

R. Yukon

Mt McKinley
6194m

Alaskan Range

R. Mackenzie

Coastal Range

R O C K Y

Vancouver Island

Vancouver

R. Snake

Sierra Nevada

Great Salt Lake

M O U N T A I N S

Great Plains

R. Missouri

San Francisco

Mt Whitney
4418m

Mt Elbert
4399m

Los Angeles

R. Colorado

Grand Canyon

Hudson Bay

Lake Superior

Lake Huron

Lake Michigan

Toronto

Lake Ontario

Lake Erie

Chicago

R. Mississippi

R. Ohio

St Lawrence

Quebec

Ottawa

Montreal

Appalachian Mts

Boston

New York

Washington D.C.

ATLANTIC OCEAN

Rio Grande

Gulf of California

Sierra Madre

PACIFIC OCEAN

Gulf of Mexico

Nassau

Havana

Pico Duarte
3175m

San Juan

Port au Prince

Santo Domingo

Kingston

Caribbean Sea

West Indies

Mexico City

Mt Citlaltepetl
5700m

Mt Popocatepetl
5452m

Belmopan

Guatemala City

San Salvador

Tegucigalpa

Managua

San Jose

Panama

miles
0   200   400   600   800
0   200 400 600 800
kilometres

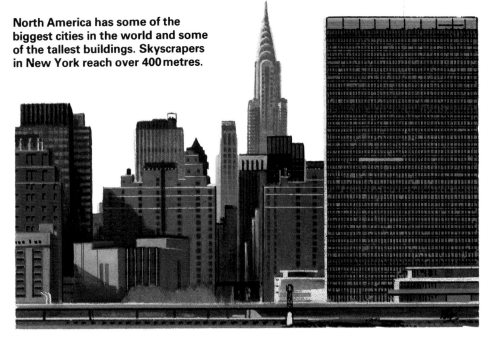

North America has some of the biggest cities in the world and some of the tallest buildings. Skyscrapers in New York reach over 400 metres.

North and Central America

North and Central America form a large land mass lying between the Pacific Ocean to the west and the Atlantic to the east. The land ranges from icy wastes in the Arctic north to tropical forests in the south near the equator. In between lie Canada's rivers and pine forests, and the flat grassy plains of the USA. Swamps are found in the south-east and deserts in the south-west.

The chief mountain range runs the length of the continent on the west. In the USA its name is the Rocky Mountains. Mexicans call it the Sierra Madre. East of the Rockies are the Great Plains, sloping down to the Gulf of Mexico lowlands in the south and reaching the Great Lakes in the north.

Water flows from the Great Lakes by way of the Niagara Falls into the Hudson River and the Atlantic. Many Canadian rivers and lakes drain into Hudson Bay, while the Mississippi and Missouri – the longest rivers on the continent – run down the Great Plains to the Gulf of Mexico. The Colorado River reaches the Pacific through the Grand Canyon, the world's largest gorge.

In the east of the continent are the Appalachian Mountains. These are the stumps of a mountain range that was once higher than the Rockies and which have been worn down by water, wind and ice over millions of years.

A drum majorette twirls her baton as she leads a marching band. Americans love a big parade, especially on 4 July to celebrate their independence.

Canada and the USA

KEY FACTS: USA

Area: 9,363,123 sq km
Population: 226,505,000
Capital: Washington, D.C.
Highest peak: Mount McKinley (6194 metres)
Longest river: Mississippi – Missouri (6230 km)

The two newest states of the USA are Alaska and Hawaii, which became full states in 1959.

The unit of money in the USA is the dollar.

The USA is the fourth largest country in the world, in size and number of people. It is also the richest and most powerful nation. Its northern neighbour is Canada, the world's second largest country. But Canada has only one tenth of the population of the USA.

Both countries were explored by the British and the French in the 1660s. Long before this, Indians from Asia had settled there. In 1783, thirteen American colonies became independent as the United States of America. Britain and France shared Canada for a time before it became British alone in 1763, and finally independent in 1867.

Canada has twelve provinces and territories. The capital is Ottawa. French and English are both spoken, and Montreal, the largest city, is mainly French-speaking. But for its vast size the country has few cities. Most Canadians live in the south, near the ports and factories around the Great Lakes and St Lawrence River. In the cold Arctic north live the Inuit (Eskimo).

Canada's head of state is Queen Elizabeth II, but the federal government is led by the prime minister. Canada produces many minerals, such as asbestos, nickel and zinc. Fruit and cereal crops, as well as cattle ranching, are also important.

The USA is made up of 50 states and the small district of Columbia, which includes the capital city of Washington. Alaska is the largest state, but California has the largest number of people. New York is the second largest city in the world, and other great cities include Chicago, Los Angeles and San Francisco. Many Americans live in the country, for farming is an important industry.

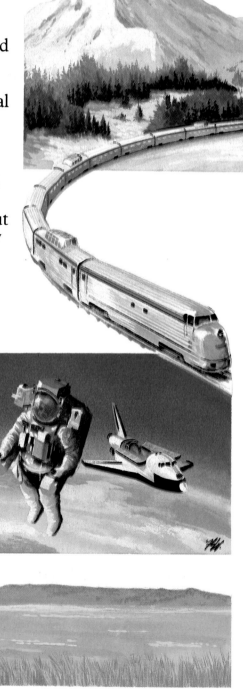

Above right: The first railway across the USA was completed in 1869. Canada was crossed in 1885. **Right:** The USA leads the world in space technology. In 1984 an American astronaut 'walked' in space for the first time without a life-line. **Below:** Teams of combine harvesters are a common sight on the vast wheatfields of the North American prairies.

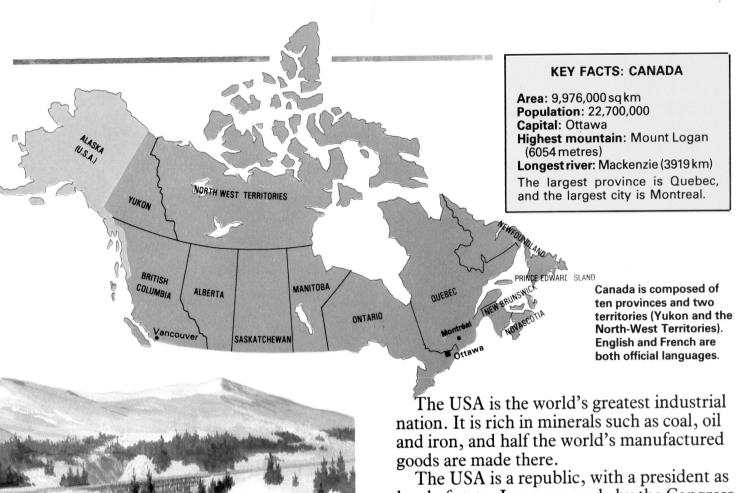

KEY FACTS: CANADA

Area: 9,976,000 sq km
Population: 22,700,000
Capital: Ottawa
Highest mountain: Mount Logan (6054 metres)
Longest river: Mackenzie (3919 km)
The largest province is Quebec, and the largest city is Montreal.

Canada is composed of ten provinces and two territories (Yukon and the North-West Territories). English and French are both official languages.

The USA is the world's greatest industrial nation. It is rich in minerals such as coal, oil and iron, and half the world's manufactured goods are made there.

The USA is a republic, with a president as head of state. Laws are made by the Congress and Senate and each state has its own government and governor.

Fifty states and the District of Columbia make up the USA. The 'Original Thirteen' states which declared their independence from Britain in 1776 were Connecticut, Delaware, Georgia, Maryland, Massachusetts, New Hampshire, New Jersey, New York, North Carolina, Pennsylvania, Rhode Island, South Carolina and Virginia.

13

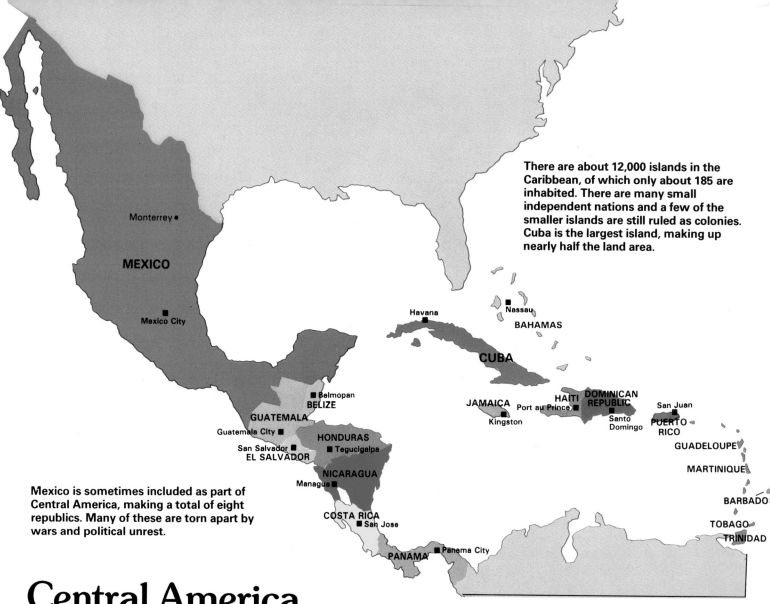

Monterrey •

MEXICO

■ Mexico City

There are about 12,000 islands in the Caribbean, of which only about 185 are inhabited. There are many small independent nations and a few of the smaller islands are still ruled as colonies. Cuba is the largest island, making up nearly half the land area.

■ Nassau
BAHAMAS

Havana ■
CUBA

■ Belmopan
BELIZE

GUATEMALA

Guatemala City ■

San Salvador ■
EL SALVADOR

HONDURAS
■ Tegucigalpa

JAMAICA   **HAITI** **DOMINICAN REPUBLIC**
Port au Prince ■
Kingston   Santo Domingo

San Juan ■
PUERTO RICO

GUADELOUPE

MARTINIQUE

NICARAGUA
Managua ■

Mexico is sometimes included as part of Central America, making a total of eight republics. Many of these are torn apart by wars and political unrest.

COSTA RICA
■ San Jose

BARBADO

TOBAGO

TRINIDAD

PANAMA   ■ Panama City

Central America and the Caribbean

Central America is a narrow strip of land joining Mexico to South America. To the east is the Caribbean Sea, where the islands of the West Indies lie.

The climate is mainly hot and moist this near to the equator, and thick tropical forests are found. In the Central American mountains, people find it too cold to live. Instead they make their homes in the upland plains, where the climate is milder.

Many volcanoes are found in this part of the world. Some are still active. Crops of coffee, sugar, bananas, tobacco, cotton and cocoa are grown in the rich volcanic soils. Most people live by farming, but the soil is also rich in minerals. In Central America gold, silver, zinc, copper, lead and iron are mined. Natural gas, petroleum and bauxite (for making aluminium) are found in the West Indies. Wood from the forests is sold abroad.

The Pan–American Highway is the main road link across Central America. The main waterway is the Panama Canal, linking the Caribbean Sea to the Pacific Ocean. This canal makes the region important for world trade and shipping.

KEY FACTS

Area: West Indies – 240,000 sq km;
Central America – 2,560,000 sq km

Central America has one of the world's fastest growing populations.

The Panama Canal is the busiest canal in the world. It is 82 km long.

Sugar cane is an important crop in the Caribbean. Machines are now used to cut the tall canes, but some are still harvested by hand.

CARIBBEAN SEA

South America

Caracas

R. Orinoco

Georgetown
Paramaribo
Cayenne

*Guiana
Highlands*

ATLANTIC
OCEAN

Bogota

Quito

R. Negro

R. Amazon

S e l v a s

Recife •

R. Purus

R. Maranon

*A
n
d
e
s*

R. Ucayali

Lima

Lake
Titicaca

R. Madeira

Mato Grosso

■ Brasilia

La Paz

Lake
Poopo

PACIFIC
OCEAN

*Brazilian
Highlands*

*M
o
u
n
t
a
i
n
s*

Atacama Desert

*G
r
a
n

C
h
a
c
o*

R. Paraguay

R. Parana

Sao Paulo • • Rio de Janeiro

Asuncion

The Amazon River, which begins
in the Peruvian Andes, has a
greater flow of water than any
other river, and drains an area of
over 7 million sq km. At its mouth
it is 80 km wide. The tropical rain
forest of the Amazon basin, called
the Selvas, is the largest in the
world.

R. Uruguay

ATLANTIC
OCEAN

▲ *Mt Aconcagua
6960m*

Santiago ■

*P
a
m
p
a
s*

R. Salado

Montevideo

Buenos Aires

South America has vast areas of
rich grasslands, such as the Llanos
of Venezuela and the Pampas of
Argentina. They are ideal for cattle
ranching. In southern Argentina
the sparse grass of the dry
Patagonian plains is better suited
to sheep ranching.

The Andes run some 7000 km from
north to south down South
America. They shield much of the
western coast from rain-bearing
winds and have created the driest
of the world's deserts, the
Atacama.

Miles
0 100 200 300 400 500

0   200 400 600 800
Kilometres

*P
a
t
a
g
o
n
i
a*

The southern tip of South America
is only about 1000 km from
Antarctica. Cold waters from the
Antarctic are carried up the west
coast by the Humboldt Current.
This keeps the temperature cool
as far north as the equator.

*Tierra
del Fuego*

Cape Horn

15

The South American continent is over 7000 kilometres long from north to south. Its northern lands are tropical. Thick rain forests and wide grassy plains are found in Central South America. But at its southern tip, the continent is bare and windswept.

The high Andes Mountains run almost the whole length of South America on the western side. Of the many rivers that rise in the Andes, the longest are the Amazon and Plata-Parana.

The huge Amazon river flows through the largest rain forest in the world. Here the climate is moist, with plenty of rain. But beyond the Andes, in the Atacama Desert of Chile, lie some of the driest spots on Earth.

Plants and Animals

Plants of many different kinds thrive in the continent's varied climates. Coffee, cocoa, sugar and bananas grow well in the tropical areas. So do other important crops such as rubber, tobacco and cotton. Many well-known food plants first came from South America. They include the potato, tomato and maize.

South America has its own collection of animals, some of which are found nowhere else in the world. Among them are the llama and armadillo, the ostrich-like rhea and the water-hog, or capybara.

The Story of South America

The first people to live in South America were American Indians, who came from Asia by way of North America. Mighty empires, such as that of the Incas in Peru, governed the continent before the first Europeans arrived in the 1400s. Spain and Portugal seized most of South America. But in the 1800s the South Americans fought off European rule and set up republics of their own. There are 14 countries in South America today. Most of the people speak Spanish. But Portuguese is the language of Brazil, the largest South American country.

Above: The fortress city of Macchu Picchu stands high in the Andes in Peru. This outpost was part of the Inca Empire that once ruled large areas of South America.

Ecuador takes its name from the Spanish word for equator, which passes through Ecuador.

Colombia was named after Christopher Columbus, the Italian explorer who landed in the Americas in 1492.

Bolivia is named after Simon Bolivar (The Liberator) who freed the country from Spanish rule in 1825.

The Land and its People

A mixture of peoples live in South America today. South American Indians are found mostly in Ecuador, Peru and Bolivia, and in remote areas of other countries. Indians in the Amazon rain forest knew nothing of the outside world until a few years ago. Now many have lost their lands as the forest has been cut down for new settlements and the building of the Trans-Amazon Highway. Others have died from diseases brought by Europeans.

Most South Americans are of mixed blood, with both Europeans and Indians among their ancestors. Some people have European ancestors only. Others have African ancestors who were brought as slaves to work on the huge farms owned by Europeans. Asians (Indians, Chinese and Indonesians) live mainly in Guyana and Surinam. More people live in Brazil than in any other South American country. And half the Brazilians live in towns and great cities such as Sao Paulo and Rio de Janeiro.

The Countries of South America

Of South America's northern lands only Venezuela is rich, from its large oilfields. Poor farmers elsewhere grow coffee, bananas, sugar-cane and cocoa.

Peru, Bolivia and Brazil cover central South America. Brazil is the world's largest producer of coffee, but it also has modern factories and valuable minerals. The continent's poorest nation is Bolivia, where mining (especially for tin) is important. Peru too relies on mining, as well as fishing.

In the south, Argentina is the biggest country. The cattle which roam its vast grassy plains, or Pampas, are tended by gauchos (cowboys). Meat and crops are the chief products. Uruguay produces meat and wool, while Chile mines large amounts of copper.

Above (top): In the Amazon rain forest a few Indians still live by hunting. The longbow and barbed arrows are a favourite weapon for catching fish. But the simple way of life of the Amazon Indian is being destroyed by the rapid development of the area.

Above: Cowhands in Argentina still wear the traditional gaucho costume – poncho, pleated trousers and long leather boots. Gauchos first rounded up the wild cattle of the Pampas almost 300 years ago.

On Lake Titicaca in the Andes live a tribe of people called the Uru. They live on floating mats of dried reeds and make reed boats called balsas.

17

Europe

Reykjavik

Note: Eastern Europe continued on page 28

miles
0   200   400   600
0   200 400 600
kilometres

Norwegian Sea

Gulf of Bothnia

Lake Onega

Lake Ladoga

S c a n d i n a v i a

Helsinki

Oslo

Stockholm

Lake Vanern

Moscow

R. Dvina

ATLANTIC OCEAN

Copenhagen

North Sea

Baltic Sea

Dublin

North European Plain

Berlin

R. Vistula

Warsaw

R. Dnieper

London

The Hague

R. Rhine

R. Elbe

Brussels

Bonn

Prague

C a r p a t h i a n   M t s

Paris

R. Seine

Luxembourg

Vosges

Vienna

Budapest

R. Loire

Berne

Hungarian Plain

Bay of Biscay

Mt Blanc 4807m

T h e   A l p s

R. Rhone

R. Po

Bucharest

Black Sea

Belgrade

R. Danube

Dinaric Alps

Pyrenees Mts

Pico de Aneto 3404m

B a l k a n   M t s

Sofia

M   e   s   e   t   a

R. Ebro

Apennine Mts

Adriatic Sea

Tirane

Lisbon

Madrid

R. Tagus

Rome

Mt Olympus 2911m

Balearic Islands

Athens

Mediterranean Sea

Mt Etna 3340m

Although Europe is the world's second smallest continent, its coastline is about 80,000 km long. A warm current called the Gulf Stream keeps northern Europe mild in winter. It comes from the Gulf of Mexico. Further north still lie the frozen lands of the Arctic where no trees grow. This region is known as tundra.

Europe forms the western part of a great land mass, most of which is taken up by Asia. Europe is the world's second smallest continent and has seas on three sides. The north coast faces the Arctic Ocean, with the Atlantic Ocean to the west. To the south are the Black Sea, the Caucasus Mountains and the warm Mediterranean Sea, which divides Europe from Africa. In the east the Caspian Sea, Ural River and Ural Mountains cut the continent off from the great plains of Asia. More people live in Europe than in any other continent apart from Asia.

Left: Grapes are grown over much of Europe, where wine is a popular drink. Many vines are planted on terraced slopes. Below: The peoples of Europe have their own languages, dress and folk customs. Today, their special dress is often worn only for festivals or displays of folk dancing.

Above: France is famous for its many beautiful chateaux. Right: Many of Europe's ideas about government and art come from the ancient Greeks. This beautiful Greek sculpture of Aphrodite is almost 2500 years old.

The Lands of Europe

Europe's great central plain stretches from the Ural Mountains to the Atlantic in the west. Highlands include the Alps of central Europe, the Pyrenees and Sierra Nevada of the south-west, the Urals in the east and the Carpathians in the south. The main rivers are the Danube, Rhine and Volga.

Europe's jagged coastline was scoured away by ice thousands of years ago during the last Ice Age. Today, northern Europe has a cool, moist climate. Snow lies in the Arctic lands for much of the year, while the Mediterranean lands are warm and dry.

The People

People have lived in Europe since earliest times. Cave paintings show them hunting the bison that roamed the land thousands of years ago.

Europe was settled by people pushing west to find good hunting. Later they cut down forests to make farmland.

Much of Europe's civilization is based on that of ancient Greece and Rome. But each nation has kept its own language and customs. Europeans have always been great sailors and traders. From the late 1400s they explored the world, spreading their ideas to new lands.

Reykjavik ICELAND

SWEDEN FINLAND
Helsinki

NORWAY
Oslo Stockholm

SCOTLAND

DENMARK
Copenhagen

RUSSIA
Moscow

UNITED
KINGDOM

Dublin
IRELAND

WALES
ENGLAND NETHERLANDS Berlin Warsaw
London Amsterdam WEST EAST POLAND
Brussels GERMANY
BELGIUM Bonn Prague
Paris Luxembourg CZECHOSLOVAKIA

Vienna Budapest
FRANCE Berne AUSTRIA HUNGARY
SWITZERLAND RUMANIA
ITALY Belgrade Bucharest
YUGOSLAVIA
BULGARIA
PORTUGAL Sofia
Madrid Rome Tirane TURKEY
Lisbon ALBANIA
SPAIN GREECE
Athens

Below right: The Rhine, Germany's longest river, flows 1300 km from its source in Switzerland to the North Sea. In Germany its banks are bordered by vineyards and castles built high on overhanging crags.

Below bottom: Europe produces many manufactured goods such as electrical equipment, cameras and machine tools. One of its most important industries is car manufacturing. Much of the work that was once done by humans is now done by robots.

Governments of Europe

The countries of Europe are mostly republics, where the head of state is an elected president. Some nations have a king, queen or prince, but few royal rulers have real control over affairs of state. Government is in the hands of a prime minister and an elected parliament. In eastern Europe there are communist governments. These states allow only one political party, so that free elections like those in western countries do not take place.

Countries belonging to the European Economic Community have their own parliament. Its members are elected to deal with the Community's affairs and they come from every member country. The parliament meets in Strasbourg, but as yet has less control over Community affairs than the EEC Commission which is based in Brussels.

European Nations

Europe is a mixture of countries, each with its own way of life and language, yet sharing a common 'European' tradition. Some countries, such as Greece, have a history thousands of years old. Others, such as Yugoslavia, came into being only after the end of the First World War in 1918. Many modern European nations have grown up since the 1500s. Up until the First World War much of the continent was in the hands of large empires, such as the Austrian and the Russian.

Languages of Europe

European languages have spread throughout the world. They fall into three main families: Germanic (such as English), Romance (such as French) and Slavic (such as Russian). Romance languages sprang from Latin, the language of the Romans. Many people speak local dialects of their national language. In some countries, groups fight to keep their own language and traditions. Among them are the Welsh, the Basques of Spain and France, and the Walloons in Belgium.

The European Community

After the Second World War, several countries of western Europe joined to form a 'common market' for their goods. The aim was to do away with trade barriers such as customs duties. They formed the European Economic Community (EEC). Today the EEC has 10 member countries. It is run by a Commission.

One of the most important products of Scandinavia is timber. The easiest method of transporting the newly felled trees is to float them downstream to the timber yards.

European History

Europe has a history of wars and quarrels between its many nations. Some leaders, such as Napoleon and Hitler, have dreamed of ruling the whole continent.

In the 20th century, two world wars (1914–18 and 1939–45) began as a result of troubles in Europe. Both wars caused great loss of life and the Second World War great damage. Today, Europe is still divided, between the West and the communist countries of the East.

The Scandinavian countries of northern Europe include Norway, Iceland, Sweden, Finland and Denmark. Dairy farming is important and other products are fish, timber, oil and manufactured goods.

Southern Europe includes Spain, Portugal and Italy. Their chief products are cereals, fruit, wine, vegetables, fish, cork, textiles and manufactured goods. Tourism is important.

Western Europe includes Ireland, the UK, France, the Netherlands, Belgium and Luxembourg. Here coal, iron and steel, oil, dairy foods, livestock, wine and manufactured goods are produced.

Central European countries are Switzerland, Liechtenstein, Czechoslovakia, Austria, West and East Germany. Engineering, chemicals, timber, wine, metal and manufactured goods are all important.

South-East Europe is often called the Balkans. Its countries are Yugoslavia, Albania, Greece and Bulgaria. They produce cereals, fruit, wine and other crops.

Eastern Europe includes Hungary, Poland, Romania, and the USSR west of the Ural Mountains. Here livestock, cereals, minerals, coal, gas, oil and manufactured goods are important.

The countries of Europe mostly belong to one of two military groups. Western countries are members of the North Atlantic Treaty Organization (NATO). Eastern nations belong to the Warsaw Pact. Some countries belong to neither and are called neutral. They include Switzerland, Sweden and Austria.

British Isles

Orkney Islands
• Kirkwall

Shetland Islands
• Lerwick

Outer Hebrides

North West Highlands

Loch Ness

• Inverness

R. Don

• Aberdeen

Ben Nevis
1344m

Grampians

R. Dee

R. Tay

Loch Lomond

Glasgow

Edinburgh

R. Tweed

SCOTLAND

Southern Uplands

Newcastle

miles
0   50   100
0   50   100
Kilometres

The seas around the British Isles have always been important fishing grounds. Today they have a new importance. Oil wells in the North Sea provide Britain with all the oil it needs.

ATLANTIC OCEAN

• Londonderry

NORTHERN IRELAND

Lough Neagh

Belfast

Slieve Donard
852m
Mourne Mts

Isle of Man

IRISH SEA

NORTH SEA

Lake District
▲ Scafell Pike
979m

Middlesbrough

Pennines

York

REPUBLIC OF IRELAND

R. Liffey

Central Plain

■ Dublin

Leeds

Liverpool   Manchester

Sheffield

R. Trent

R. Shannon

R. Barrow

Wicklow Mts

Nottingham

The Wash

Limerick

R. Dee

Mt. Snowdon
1085m

The Fens

Carrantuohill
1041m

• Cork

Cambrian Mts

R. Severn

• Birmingham

ENGLAND

• Cambridge

St. George's Channel

WALES

Oxford

London ■

• Swansea

Cardiff • Bristol

R. Thames   North Downs

• Dover

For their size the British Isles have an amazing variety of scenery, ranging from the rolling hills of southern England, through the flat plains of the Fens and the craggy peaks of the Lake District to the ancient mountains of Scotland and Wales.

Exmoor

Southampton   South Downs

English Channel

Dartmoor

Isle of Wight

Plymouth

Isles of Scilly

Channel Islands

The British Isles lie between the Atlantic Ocean and the North Sea. They are divided from the north coast of Europe by the English Channel. The islands are split between two countries – the Republic of Ireland and the United Kingdom of England, Scotland, Wales and Northern Ireland.

Many landscapes make up this small group of islands. Scotland, Wales, Ireland and north-west England have most of the uplands and lakes. But the highest mountain, Ben Nevis, reaches only 1343 metres. Sheep are kept on the hills, especially on the country's wetter west side. Cereals are grown in the fertile soils of the east, especially in East Anglia.

Areas of moorland are found in the south-west and north-east. Down the centre of northern England runs the Pennine Chain of hills, while the Cheviot Hills mark the border with Scotland. The beautiful Scottish Highlands are popular with tourists.

Ireland is divided from the rest of the British Isles by sea. Northern Ireland is mainly hilly. Most of the Republic is a low-lying plain, through which flows the River Shannon.

Left: Tourism is an important industry in the United Kingdom, and the Tower of London is a popular attraction. Started soon after the Norman conquest, it has served as both a prison and a royal residence.

Above: Oil from the North Sea is piped ashore to Britain. Working on the platform means spending weeks at a time on the rig.

Left: A typical English scene – a village green with a cricket match in progress. Sport is a popular British pastime and many international games originated in this country.

KEY FACTS: UNITED KINGDOM

Area: 244,046 sq km
Population: 55,822,000
Capital: London
Highest mountain: Ben Nevis (1344 metres)
Longest river: Severn (336 km)

Smaller islands in the British Isles group include the Isle of Man (527 sq km) and the Channel Islands.

REPUBLIC OF IRELAND

Area: 70,283 sq km
Population: 3,236,000
Capital: Dublin
Highest mountain: Carrantuohill (1041 metres)
Longest river: Shannon (350 km)

Farms and Factories

The United Kingdom grows much of its own food, but few people work on farms. Most live and work in the industrial cities of London, the Midlands and the North, as well as Glasgow and Swansea. Ireland relies mainly on dairy farming.

The United Kingdom was the world's first industrial nation. The traditional shipbuilding, engineering and coal-mining industries are now being replaced by new ones such as electronics. The country has rich reserves of coal, iron-ore, oil and natural gas. Banking is also important.

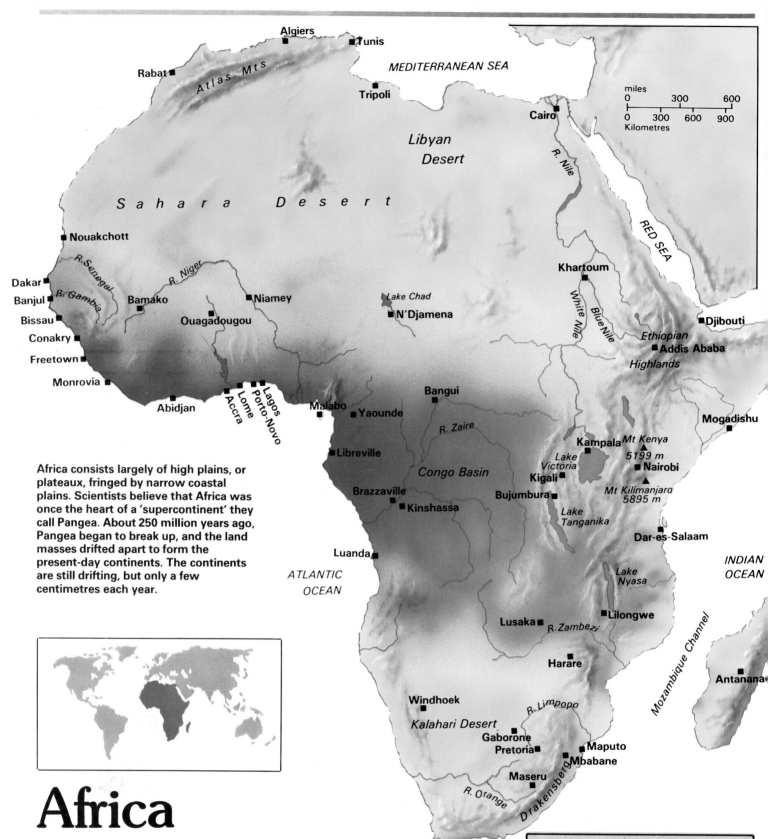

Algiers
Tunis
MEDITERRANEAN SEA
Rabat
Atlas Mts
Tripoli
Cairo
Libyan
Desert
R. Nile
miles
0   300   600
0   300   600   900
Kilometres
RED SEA
Sahara   Desert
Nouakchott
R. Senegal
Khartoum
Dakar
R. Niger
White Nile
Blue Nile
Banjul
R. Gambia
Bamako
Niamey
Lake Chad
Ethiopian
Djibouti
Bissau
Ouagadougou
N'Djamena
Highlands
Addis Ababa
Conakry
Freetown
Monrovia
Lagos
Abidjan
Porto-Novo
Lome
Accra
Malabo
Bangui
Mogadishu
Yaounde
R. Zaire
Libreville
Kampala
Mt Kenya
5199 m
Lake
Victoria
Nairobi
Africa consists largely of high plains, or
plateaux, fringed by narrow coastal
plains. Scientists believe that Africa was
once the heart of a 'supercontinent' they
call Pangea. About 250 million years ago,
Pangea began to break up, and the land
masses drifted apart to form the
present-day continents. The continents
are still drifting, but only a few
centimetres each year.
Congo Basin
Kigali
Brazzaville
Bujumbura
Mt Kilimanjaro
5895 m
Kinshassa
Lake
Tanganika
Luanda
Dar-es-Salaam
INDIAN
OCEAN
ATLANTIC
OCEAN
Lake
Nyasa
Lilongwe
Lusaka
R. Zambezi
Harare
Mozambique Channel
Antananarivo
Windhoek
R. Limpopo
Kalahari Desert
Gaborone
Pretoria
Maputo
Mbabane
Maseru
Drakensberg
R. Orange

Africa

Africa is the world's second largest continent and is joined to
Asia by a thin strip of land north of the Red Sea. But across
this land runs the Suez Canal, so that the continent is
surrounded by water.

North Africa faces the Mediterranean Sea. To the west is
the Atlantic Ocean, with the Indian Ocean to the east. The
large island of Madagascar lies off the east coast.

Most of Africa falls within the tropics and has a warm
climate. A high plain, or tableland, covers most of the

KEY FACTS

Area: 30,319,000 sq km
Population: 442,000,000
Highest peak: Mount Kilimanjaro
 (5895 metres)
Longest river: Nile (6679 km)

Africa is the world's second largest
continent.

The River Nile is the longest river in
the world, and the Sahara is the
largest desert.

continent. Mountains and deserts lie to the north and north-east, with grassy plains and hills to the south. In the west there are thick rain forests.

The Great Rift Valley runs down the east of Africa, from north to south. It includes the continent's highest peaks – Mounts Kilimanjaro and Kenya – both of which are dead volcanoes. Parts of the Valley have filled with water to become huge lakes. The greatest of the African lakes is Victoria, which is the third largest in the world.

Great rivers rise in central Africa and the eastern mountains. They include the Zaire, Niger, Zambezi and the Nile, which is the longest. Few goods are carried by river because of the many waterfalls and rapids along their course.

Deserts and Grasslands

Much of Africa is desert and the largest desert area is the Sahara. Countries to its north have the warm climate of Mediterranean lands. To its south the lands are much hotter and drier, so that few crops can be grown. In the south-west lie more deserts – the Namib and Kalahari.

The grassy savannah plains south of the Sahara and the high veldt of South Africa are rich in wildlife. On the rolling grasslands roam elephants, leopards, cheetahs and antelope. In the forests live gorillas and chimpanzees. Crocodiles and hippopotamuses are found in the rivers.

The Wealth of the Land

The crops of Africa include palm oil, peanuts, cocoa, cotton, millet, dates, fruits, maize and yams. The forests provide timber, and fishing is also important. Herds of cattle, sheep and goats are kept by farmers. Africa also has great mineral wealth. Gold, diamonds, copper and phosphates for fertilizers are among mining products. Oil has been found in some areas.

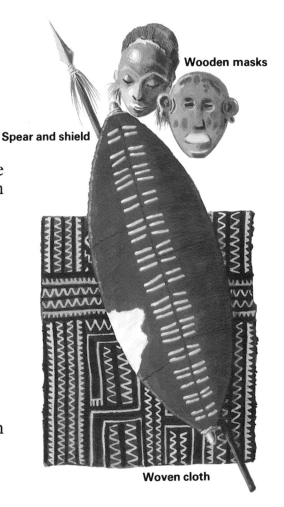

Wooden masks

Spear and shield

Woven cloth

Above: Wood carving is a favourite African art form. Bold patterns are often used in decoration and weaving.

Below: The African grasslands once supported a rich variety of large mammals. Today these animals are mainly confined to game reserves, some of which are the size of small European countries.

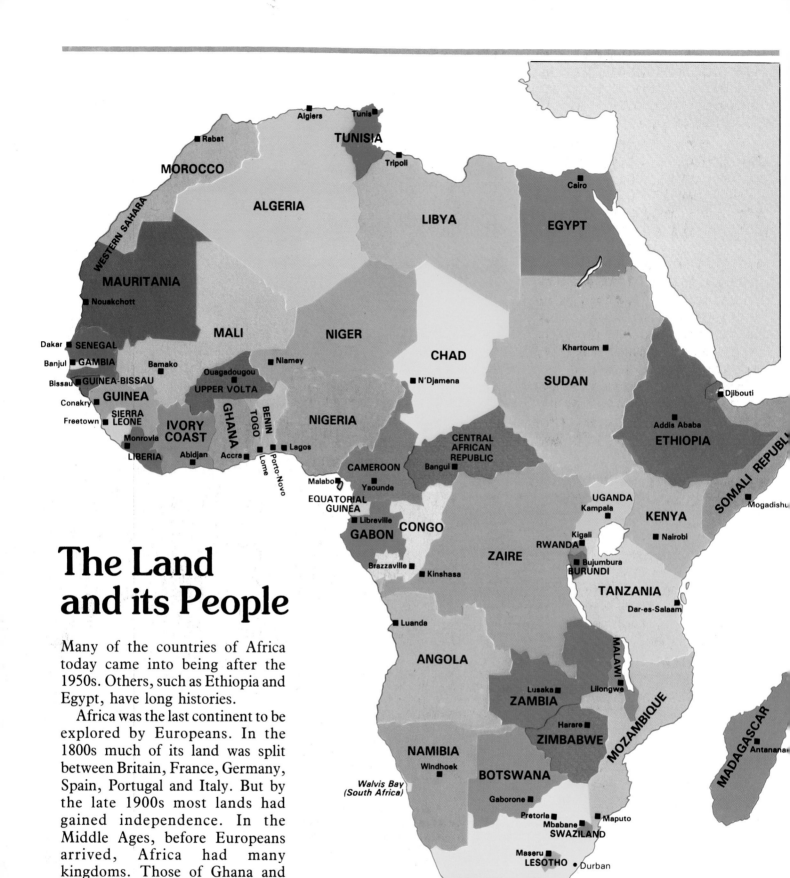

The Land and its People

Many of the countries of Africa today came into being after the 1950s. Others, such as Ethiopia and Egypt, have long histories.

Africa was the last continent to be explored by Europeans. In the 1800s much of its land was split between Britain, France, Germany, Spain, Portugal and Italy. But by the late 1900s most lands had gained independence. In the Middle Ages, before Europeans arrived, Africa had many kingdoms. Those of Ghana and Mali gave their names to modern countries.

The African Regions

Africa can be divided into five areas. The northern states are mainly Arab, where people follow the religion of Islam. In the Saharan states live Arab nomads, or Berbers. But in the southern parts

In 1914 Ethiopia was the only independent country in the whole of Africa. The rest of the continent was divided up between the European Powers. Today nearly every African country has gained independence. But the country borders are normally those of the old colonies, and they often cut across tribal groups or include several tribes. This has led to much unrest in newly independent countries and to bitter civil wars, some of which continue at present.

of these countries the peoples are black Africans. People of the East African countries are mostly Christian or Muslim, but some still follow local religions.

West Africa also has Christians and Muslims. This large area is divided between many countries, where people speak many languages – in Nigeria there are 250. The people here are black Africans, as they are in the Central and South African states. Some of these nations, such as Angola, Mozambique and Zimbabwe, were among the last to gain independence. South Africa is still ruled by a white government, while most of its people are black.

Most African countries are republics. Some, such as Guinea, have communist governments. Most people live by farming and mining.

Famine

Most of the people in Africa farm the land or herd animals. But in many places the soil is too poor or the rainfall too little for crops to grow well. As a result there are many poor people in Africa.

One of the worst areas for droughts is the huge grassland south of the Sahara – the Sahel. In recent years there has been so little rain that many thousands of people have starved to death as their crops have withered, and millions of domestic animals have perished. Aid has been given to the Sahel, but nothing can stop the droughts.

Above: In many parts of Africa cattle are counted as wealth. These hump-backed zebu thrive on poor grass and withstand heat and insects.

Above right: South Africa is a treasure-chest of minerals, particularly gold. Some of the gold mines are over 3 kilometres deep.

The Great Sphinx, like the Pyramids, was built by the Egyptians thousands of years ago.

Below: Egypt has been called 'the gift of the Nile' because crops can only be grown through irrigation – the watering of the land. Water is raised from the Nile, sometimes by means of a bucket on a long pole, and carried through the fields by channels.

ARCTIC OCEAN

R. Lena

Siberian Plain

R. Ob

R. Yenisey

■ Moscow

R. Volga

Lake Baikal

Ural Mountains

Black Sea

Altai Mts

■ Ulan Bator

Ankara ■

Mt Elbrus
5633 m
▲

Caspian
Sea

Aral
Sea

Lake Balkhash

Gobi Desert

Caucasus Mts

■ Nicosia

▲ Mt Ararat
5165m

Tien Shan

Beirut ■
Jerusalem ■ ■ Damascus
■ Amman

R. Euphrates

R. Tigris

■ Baghdad

■
Tehran

▲ Mt Communism
7495m

Kunlun Shan

Kabul ■

Hindu Kush

▲ Mt K2
8611m

Plateau of Tibet

Islamabad ■

H
i
m
a
l
a
y
a
s

Zagros Mts

Persian Gulf

Riyadh ■

Abu Dhabi

R. Indus

Delhi
■

Katmandu ■
R. Ganges

Mt Everest ▲
8848m

R. Brahmaputra

Assam

Muscat ■

Rub al Khali

■ Dacca

San'a ■

Arabian Sea

Calcutta ■

Han

Aden ■

Bombay ●

D
e
c
c
a
n

Vientia

miles
0   200   400   600   800

0   200 400 600 800
kilometres

Bay of Bengal

Rangoon ■

Bangkok ■

Phnom
Penh

Colombo ■

INDIAN OCEAN

Kuala
Lumpur ■

Singapore ●

28

Jakarta

Asia

The continent of Asia covers a third of all the land on Earth and is home to half the world's people. It belongs to the same land mass as Europe, but its climate ranges from Arctic cold to tropical heat. To its east lies the Pacific Ocean. Its western border runs south from the Ural Mountains of Europe to the Arabian Peninsula.

Asia's highlands include the Himalayas, the Tien Shan, the Kunlun Shan and the Hindu Kush ranges. Between such high mountains lie the great Asian plains. The biggest of these are the plains of Mongolia and Tibet, the latter being the largest plain in the world. In the central mountains and plains rise many of Asia's longest rivers – the Indus, Ganges, Brahmaputra, Mekong, Yangtze and the Hwang Ho.

Beyond the mountain barriers stretch vast arid regions such as the Gobi and Ordos deserts. South-west Asia has hot, burning deserts, rich in oil. South-east Asia is tropical, with volcanic islands and coral reefs.

Central Asia has some of the driest places on Earth. Yet Cherrapunji in Assam is the wettest place in the world. Asia's climate is most affected by the monsoon, which brings cool dry winds in winter and hot wet winds in summer.

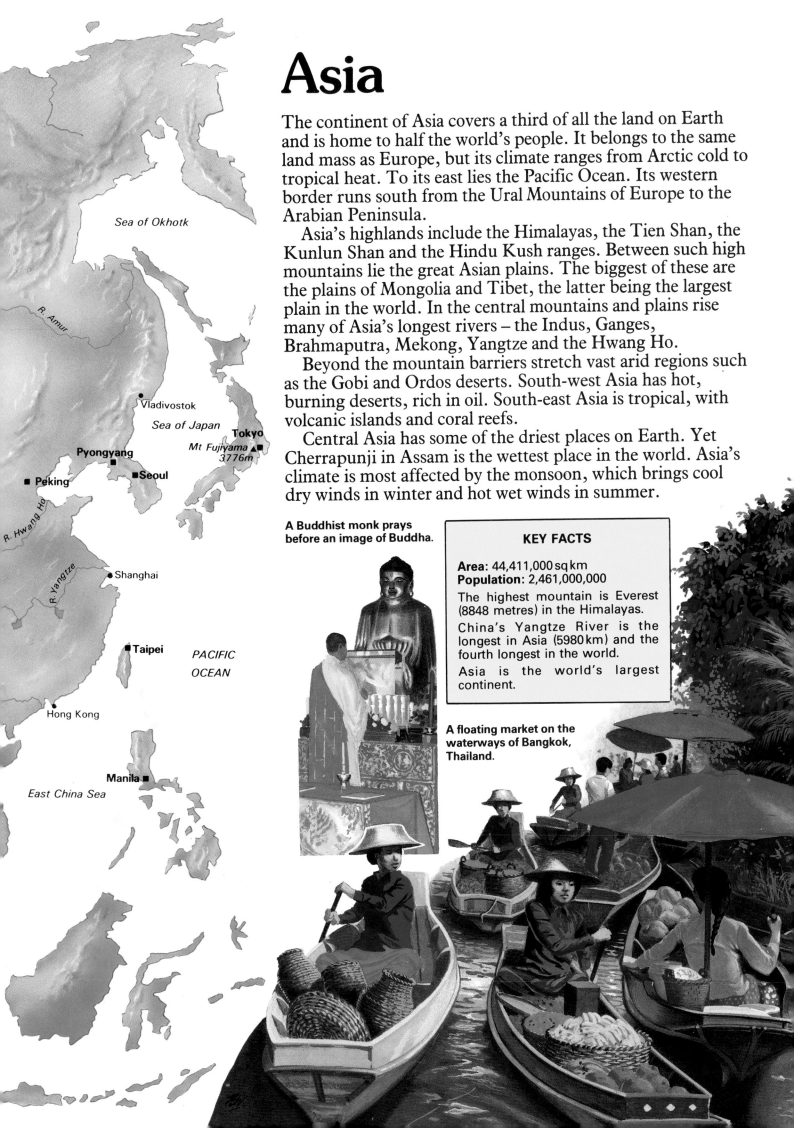

Sea of Okhotk

R. Amur

Vladivostok

Sea of Japan

Tokyo
Mt Fujiyama ▲
3776m

Pyongyang

Peking

Seoul

R. Hwang Ho

R. Yangtze

Shanghai

Taipei

PACIFIC
OCEAN

Hong Kong

Manila

East China Sea

A Buddhist monk prays
before an image of Buddha.

KEY FACTS

Area: 44,411,000 sq km
Population: 2,461,000,000

The highest mountain is Everest (8848 metres) in the Himalayas.

China's Yangtze River is the longest in Asia (5980 km) and the fourth longest in the world.

Asia is the world's largest continent.

A floating market on the waterways of Bangkok, Thailand.

The USSR

The USSR is the largest country in the world, with the third largest number of people. Its full name is the Union of Soviet Socialist Republics. Fifteen republics make up this vast and powerful nation.

The country stretches from Europe in the west to Asia in the east. Most people live in the west. Here too are most of the large industrial cities, and the best farmland. The lands of the USSR vary from frozen wastes in the north to hot deserts in the south. Across the country flow long rivers, such as the Volga, Dnieper and Yenisey. High mountains include the Ural and Tien Shan ranges. The Caspian and Aral seas are great inland lakes. Pine forests cover huge areas of Siberia, one of the coldest places on Earth. Yet the USSR also includes the hot Kara Kum Desert in central Asia. Few people live in the harsh climates of these regions.

The People
Over 100 different peoples live in the USSR. From the largest group, the Russians, comes the name by which the country is often known. In the snowy northern wilderness, only a few hunters and herdsmen live. In the far east live Asiatic people. The southern regions, such as Georgia, are famous for their folk dances. And from the Ukraine come the Cossacks, whose soldiers were once the pride of the Russian army.

Russia: The Industrial Giant
Until the 1917 revolution, Russia was a backward country of peasant farmers, ruled by an emperor, or tsar. After 1917 the communists seized power and took all lands and factories into government hands. Today the USSR rivals the USA as the strongest nation on Earth, with great industries fed by vast supplies of oil, coal and natural gas.

Engineering, textile and chemical industries are all important, and the USSR produces a fifth of the world's steel. The space and nuclear industries are also growing. But many people still work on farms.

Above: Many Mongols still live as they have done for hundreds of years, as herdsmen on the windswept plains. They live in round felt tents called yurts, made of animal hair or skins. They are expert riders and take great pride in their horses, which are a sign of wealth. They sometimes make a drink called kumys from the mare's milk.

Above right: Like the Mongols, the Cossacks of south-west Russia are also renowned for their horsemanship. During the days of the Russian Empire all Cossacks of the age of 18 were compelled to join the army for 20 years. In return for this they were granted special privileges. They were fierce fighters and many served as the Tsar's bodyguards. Some of their traditions and customs survive today, though since the revolution they have lost all their privileges.

ASIA

UNION OF SOVIET SOCIALIST REPUBLICS

erdlovsk

• Novosibirsk

AZAKHASTAN

■ Ulan Bator

Vladivostok

MONGOLIA

KIRGIZIA

OZHIKISTAN

Mongolia

In the heart of Asia, sandwiched between the USSR and China, lie the rolling plains of Mongolia.

Officially called the Mongolian People's Republic, it has been a communist state since 1921 and is allied to the USSR. The country is peopled mainly by nomadic herdsmen who wander across the dry scrublands with herds of horses, camels and sheep.

The Mongols are famous for their riding skills. In the Middle Ages fierce Mongol warriors on horseback swept across Asia and parts of Europe, burning and pillaging villages which lay in their path.

Sport and the arts are important in the USSR. Large crowds visit the Lenin Stadium to see the sporting events.

KEY FACTS: USSR

Area: 22,402,000 sq km
Population: 270,000,000
Capital: Moscow
Highest peak: Mount Communism (7495 metres)
Longest river: Ob (5410 km)

The USSR covers a sixth of the Earth's land surface.

A quarter of the USSR is in Europe; the rest is in Asia. The Ural Mountains divide the two parts.

Twelve seas flow around the USSR's coast.

MONGOLIA

Area: 1,565,000 sq km
Population: 1,835,000
Capital: Ulan Bator

In the heart of Moscow is Red Square. Red (krasnyi) once meant 'beautiful' in Russian, and the square lives up to its name. On one side stands St Basil's Cathedral with its onion shaped domes (above). On another side is Lenin's tomb. Military parades are sometimes held in the square. The USSR has a powerful army, navy and air force.

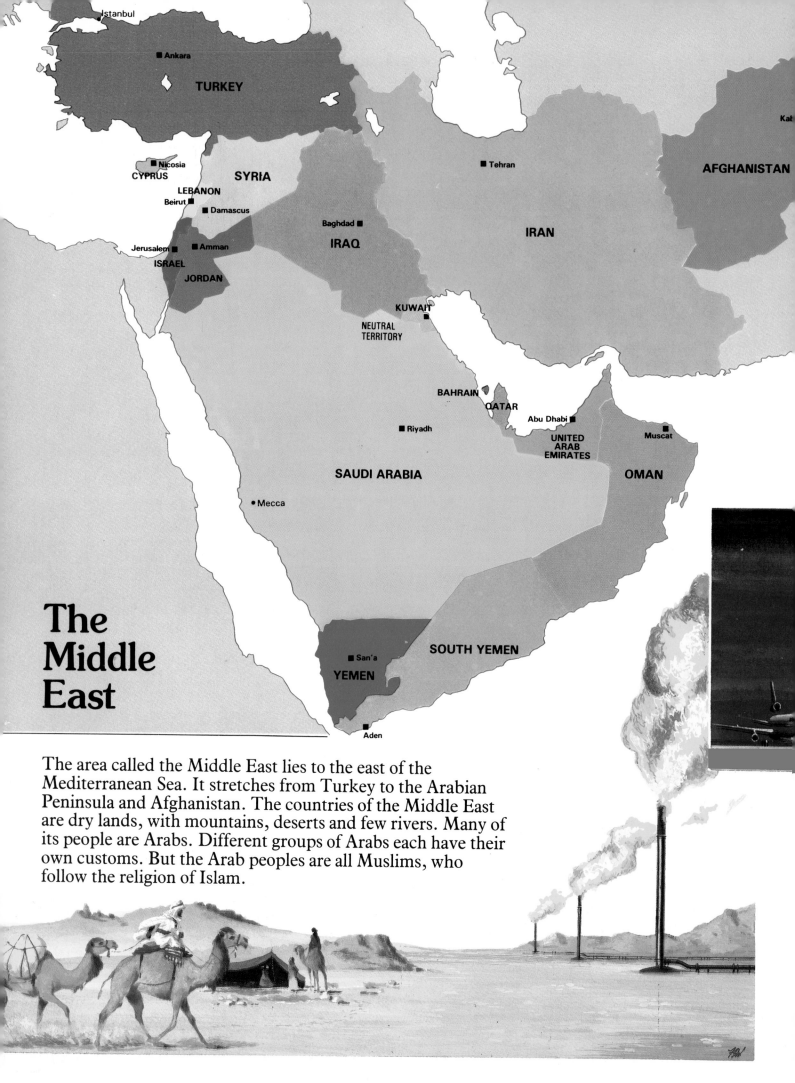

TURKEY

Istanbul

Ankara

CYPRUS

Nicosia

SYRIA

LEBANON

Beirut

Damascus

Jerusalem

Amman

ISRAEL

JORDAN

IRAQ

Baghdad

Tehran

IRAN

AFGHANISTAN

Kał

KUWAIT

NEUTRAL
TERRITORY

BAHRAIN

QATAR

Abu Dhabi

UNITED
ARAB
EMIRATES

Muscat

Riyadh

SAUDI ARABIA

OMAN

Mecca

SOUTH YEMEN

San'a

YEMEN

Aden

The Middle East

The area called the Middle East lies to the east of the
Mediterranean Sea. It stretches from Turkey to the Arabian
Peninsula and Afghanistan. The countries of the Middle East
are dry lands, with mountains, deserts and few rivers. Many of
its people are Arabs. Different groups of Arabs each have their
own customs. But the Arab peoples are all Muslims, who
follow the religion of Islam.

In most of the Middle East the soil is too poor and dry to grow crops. The best farmland lies in what is known as the 'fertile crescent', which stretches from the Mediterranean to the Tigris and Euphrates river valleys. Farmers here can grow cotton, coffee, dates, rice, tobacco, fruits, vegetables and cereals. Date palms also thrive near wells and oases. But

KEY FACTS

Saudi Arabia is the world's third largest producer of oil.

Seven small kingdoms of the Persian Gulf are joined together as the United Arab Emirates. The largest of these are Abu Dhabi and Dubai.

Languages spoken in the Middle East include Arabic, Herbrew, Persian and Turkish.

Wars

The Middle East is a troubled area of the world. In recent years wars have been fought between Iran and Iraq, and between Muslims and Christians in Lebanon. Afghanistan was invaded by the USSR in 1979. Both the USSR and the USA take a great interest in the Middle East as its oil supplies are vital to western countries.

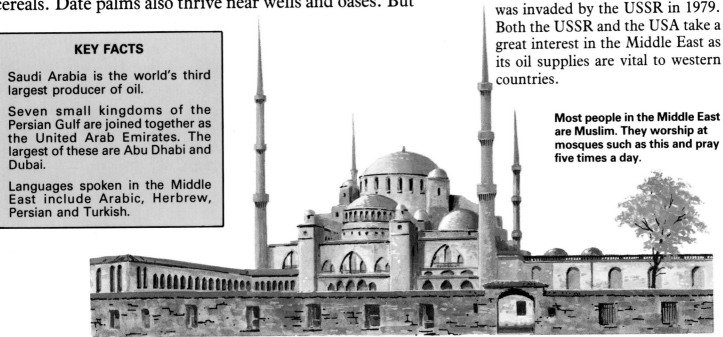

Most people in the Middle East are Muslim. They worship at mosques such as this and pray five times a day.

Opposite page: Oil has made certain Middle Eastern countries very wealthy. Yet in many areas the camel is still the major form of transport. Above: Modern airports in the oil-rich countries grow busier every year as the Middle East becomes more highly developed.

elsewhere most farmers keep animals for meat, milk and hides. Nomads herd sheep, goats and camels across the hot desert to find water and pasture at an oasis.

The Wealth of Oil

Today, old ways of life are changing quickly, for beneath the desert lie huge amounts of oil. Oil is sold abroad to fuel cars and factories, and has brought riches to the Middle East. The money helps to build roads, schools, factories and irrigation plants to bring water to the desert. Yet in countries without oil, such as Afghanistan and Yemen, the people remain poor.

Religions and Unrest

This area of Asia is home to three world religions – Judaism, Christianity and Islam. Most Israelis are Jews. In 1948 the state of Israel was set up as a homeland for the Jews. War with the Arab countries followed, for the Arabs of Palestine lost their lands when Israel was formed. Today these Arabs want a homeland for themselves. Wars between the Arabs and Israelis were fought in 1956, 1967 and 1973, and there have been many other minor conflicts.

Middle Eastern Governments

Many Middle East states are ruled by a king and royal family. Some rulers are called sheiks, sultans or emirs. Afghanistan is now a republic, as are Iraq, Yemen, Israel, Lebanon, Syria and Turkey. Iran is called an Islamic republic. Its religious leaders led a revolt against the Shah, Iran's ruler, in 1979. They feared that Iran was growing too 'westernized' and now rule the country strictly by the laws of Islam.

The Indian Sub-Continent and South-East

The Indian sub-continent is a triangle of land lying between the Arabian Sea and the Bay of Bengal. To the north rise the Himalayas, with some of the world's highest mountains.

South-East Asia includes the island nations and coastal lands which lie east of India, north of Australia and south of China. The climate here is hot and wet. Dense forest, mountains and volcanoes cover much of the land, as do many flooded rice fields. In the mountains to the north rise some of Asia's great rivers – the Irrawaddy, Salween and Mekong.

KEY FACTS:
INDIAN SUB-CONTINENT

Area: 4,488,938 sq km
Population: 750,810,000
Highest mountain: Everest (8848 metres)
Longest river: Indus (3180 km)

The countries of the sub-continent include Bangladesh, Bhutan, India, Nepal, Pakistan and Sri Lanka.

The chief products are textiles, tea, leather, manganese, iron-ore, timber, sugar, cereals and tobacco.

SOUTH-EAST ASIA

Area: 4,480,691 sq km
Population: 347,000,000
Highest mountain: Jaya (5030 metres)
Longest river: Mekong (4500 km)

The countries of South-East Asia include Brunei, Burma, Indonesia, Kampuchea, Laos, Malaysia, Singapore, Philippines, Thailand and Vietnam.

The chief products are rubber, timber, oil, fish, coconuts, tin and rice.

PHILIPPINES

Farming in the Indian Sub-Continent

Most people on the Indian sub-continent live by farming. In the Himalayan foothills of Assam and Darjeeling, tea is grown. Melting snows from the Himalayas feed India's chief rivers – the Indus, Ganges and Brahmaputra. They flow through the Punjab plains, where farmers need the water for their crops. Little rain falls on the dry, dusty plains. But when monsoon winds bring the wet season, rice, sugar and jute can be grown.

In the south is the great plain of the Deccan. The highlands of this area include the Eastern and Western Ghats. Cotton, rice, coffee, tea, rubber, millet, spices and fruits are grown in south India. Its forests produce timber and bamboo.

The People

Many peoples live on the Indian sub-continent and they speak many languages. Religion is important. In Pakistan and Bangladesh the people are mainly Muslims. In India most are Hindus, with some Sikhs, Buddhists, Jains and Parsees. Large cities such as Karachi, Calcutta, New Delhi and Bombay are over-crowded. But most people still live in small villages.

The sub-continent has been part of various empires, including the Muslim, Mogul and British. British rule ended in 1947, when India and Pakistan came into being. Pakistan was in two parts and in 1971, East Pakistan became Bangladesh. The countries of the sub-continent find it hard to feed their huge numbers of people. But new farming methods and industries are helping to improve their way of life.

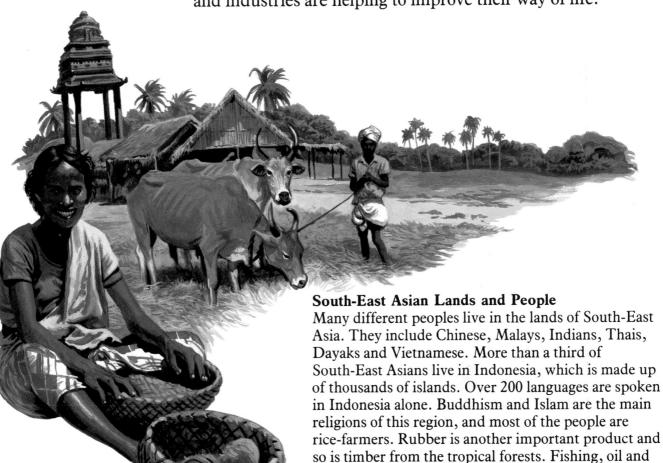

South-East Asian Lands and People

Many different peoples live in the lands of South-East Asia. They include Chinese, Malays, Indians, Thais, Dayaks and Vietnamese. More than a third of South-East Asians live in Indonesia, which is made up of thousands of islands. Over 200 languages are spoken in Indonesia alone. Buddhism and Islam are the main religions of this region, and most of the people are rice-farmers. Rubber is another important product and so is timber from the tropical forests. Fishing, oil and tin-mining are the other chief industries.

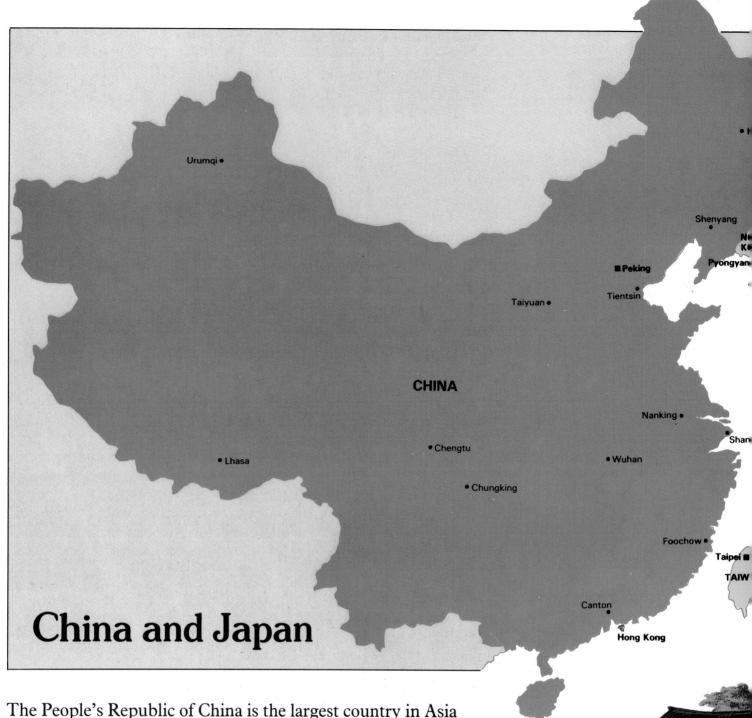

Urumqi •

Shenyang •

■ Peking

Tientsin

Taiyuan •

Pyongyan

N
K •

CHINA

Nanking •

Shan

• Chengtu

• Wuhan

• Lhasa

• Chungking

Foochow •

Taipei ■

TAIW

Canton •

Hong Kong

China and Japan

The People's Republic of China is the largest country in Asia
and the third largest in the world. It has more people than any
other nation. Most live in the east, farming the fertile valleys
of the Yangtze and Hwang Ho rivers. Much of western China
is covered by mountain ranges and other vast empty areas
include the Gobi Desert in the north.

China is divided into huge provinces ruled from the capital,
Peking (Beijing). Large factories are found in Peking and
other big cities such as Shanghai and Tientsin. Iron and steel
are their main products. China is rich in minerals, especially
coal. But most people still live by farming. More rice is grown
than in any other country. Wheat, tobacco, soya beans,
peanuts and cotton are other crops.

The Story of China

China's history goes back 4000 years. The country was ruled
by emperors until 1912, when it became a republic. In 1949 a
Communist revolution was led by Mao Tse-tung (Mao

KEY FACTS: CHINA

Area: 9,560,900 sq km
Population: 1,008,000,000
Capital: Peking (Beijing)
Longest river: Yangtze (5980 km)

China's chief products are rice,
cereals, sugar-cane, fruits, sheep,
pigs, coal, iron-ore, oil and textiles.

Zedong). The Communists began to modernize China, where hunger and disease were common and most of the people poor. The government took over all property–land, factories and mines. To improve farming, villages were grouped into communes which shared work and produce.

The Islands of Japan

Japan is a nation of islands. Its four main islands and 3000 smaller ones lie between the Sea of Japan and the Pacific Ocean. To the west is the Asian mainland. The land is mountainous, with many active volcanoes. Fujiyama, the most famous, is sacred to many Japanese.

Much of the land is forested, leaving only a small area for farming. Yet heavy crops are produced. Rice is chiefly grown and is the main food of the people, along with fish.

Most Japanese live in the large industrialized cities. Tokyo, the capital, is the largest city in the world. Japan is the most industrialized nation in Asia. But it buys many raw materials, such as oil, from abroad. Many industries were started after 1945. Today Japan is the world's leading producer of radios, televisions and video equipment, motorcycles and electronic goods. Shipbuilding and steelmaking are also important.

Left: Hong Kong harbour at sunset. This small island just off the coast of China has been a British colony since 1841. It is the centre of world trade in the Far East. It is also an important centre of international air travel.

Modern Japan is a leading producer of manufactured goods such as televisions, cameras and cars. But traditional life still goes on in homes and temples. Pagodas are common throughout China and Japan. They are a part of a temple, and serve as a shrine. The martial arts, including judo and karate, are popular in the Far East and have been practiced for hundreds of years.

KEY FACTS: JAPAN

Area: 372,313 sq km
Population: 119,000,000
Capital: Tokyo
Highest peak: Mount Fujiyama (3776 metres)
Longest river: Shinano (367 km)

Japan's chief products are rice, potatoes, cereals, fruits, textiles, steel, ships, cars, motorcycles and electrical equipment.

Honshu is Japan's largest island. The other main islands are Hokkaido, Shikoku and Kyushu.

Japan has many volcanoes. It also suffers from earthquakes, tidal waves and strong winds called typhoons.

Australia

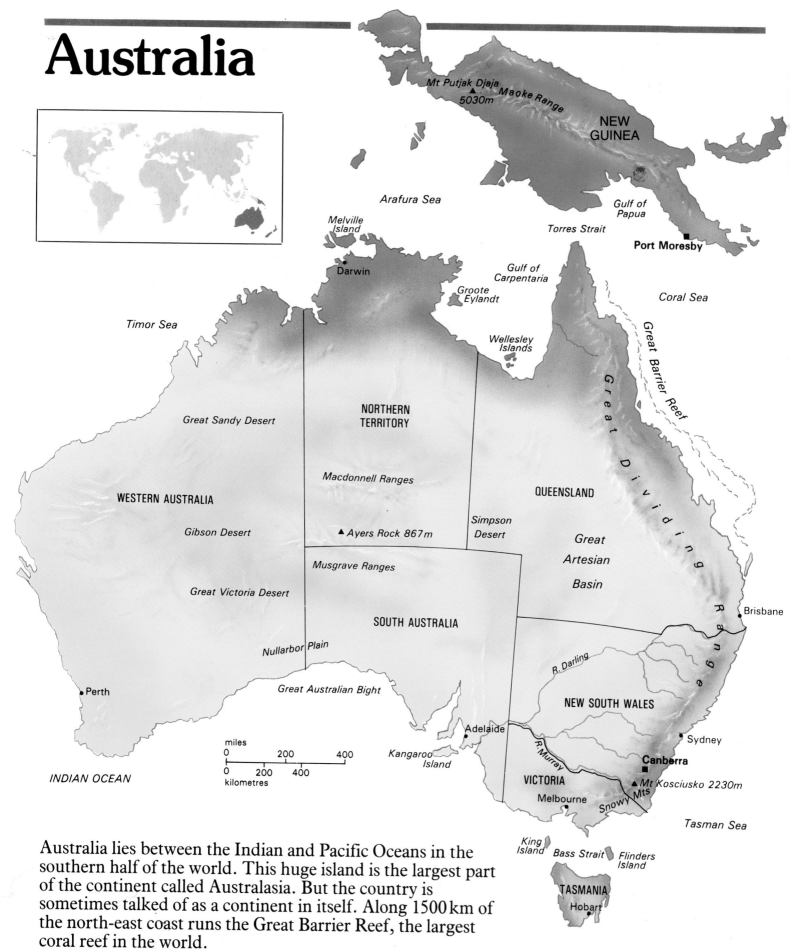

Mt Putjak Djaja
5030m
Maoke Range

NEW GUINEA

Arafura Sea

Melville Island

Gulf of Papua

Torres Strait

Port Moresby

Coral Sea

Gulf of Carpentaria

Darwin

Groote Eylandt

Wellesley Islands

Timor Sea

Great Barrier Reef

Great Sandy Desert

NORTHERN TERRITORY

WESTERN AUSTRALIA

Macdonnell Ranges

QUEENSLAND

Gibson Desert

▲ Ayers Rock 867m

Simpson Desert

Great Artesian Basin

Musgrave Ranges

Great Victoria Desert

SOUTH AUSTRALIA

Great Dividing Range

Nullarbor Plain

R. Darling

Brisbane

Great Australian Bight

Perth

NEW SOUTH WALES

miles
0   200   400

0   200   400
kilometres

Adelaide

Kangaroo Island

R. Murray

Sydney

Canberra

INDIAN OCEAN

VICTORIA

▲ Mt Kosciusko 2230m

Melbourne

Snowy Mts

Tasman Sea

King Island

Bass Strait

Flinders Island

TASMANIA

Hobart

Australia lies between the Indian and Pacific Oceans in the southern half of the world. This huge island is the largest part of the continent called Australasia. But the country is sometimes talked of as a continent in itself. Along 1500 km of the north-east coast runs the Great Barrier Reef, the largest coral reef in the world.

The great Australian land mass is mostly flat desert, for the dry western plains cover two thirds of the land. In the east are mountains and river valleys. Here, along the east and southern coasts, most Australians live.

Australia is about the size of the USA excluding Alaska, but it contains only as many people as the Netherlands – one of Europe's smaller countries. Much of the land is scrub and desert.

A lone sandstone mountain called Ayers Rock stands in central Australia. Red by day, it turns deep purple at dusk. To Aborigines the rock is sacred.

Below: The imaginative lines of the Sydney Opera House have made it one of the best known modern buildings.

The Eastern Highlands, or Great Dividing Range, run from north to south and include Mount Kosciusko, Australia's highest peak. In these mountains rise the Murray and Darling rivers, whose waters are used to irrigate crops. Farmers of the east and south-east highlands keep sheep and cattle. Huge cattle herds are also found in the dry central plains, in the area called the Great Artesian Basin. Here wells are drilled deep underground to tap water in the rock. The water provides enough pasture for grazing.

Australia is rich in minerals. Mines produce bauxite, iron, copper, gold, lead and coal; oil is produced from offshore wells in the Bass Strait.

The People

The first people to live in Australia were the Aborigines. They came from Asia, crossing the land bridge that once joined Australia to New Guinea. The Aborigines lived by hunting, fishing and gathering roots and fruits. Today, only a few still follow the traditional ways.

The Dutch found Australia in the 1600s, but the British were the first to settle there. After Captain James Cook had mapped the east coast, a prison colony was set up by the British in 1788, on the spot where the city of Sydney now stands. Many more settlers came after gold was found in the 1800s. Most Australians now live in towns, half of them in the cities of Sydney, Melbourne, Brisbane and Adelaide.

Australia is divided into six states and two territories, each with its own government. The central government meets in the capital, Canberra. It is led by the prime minister.

Left: Many marsupial animals (mammals which carry their young in a pouch) live in Australia. They include kangaroos and tree-dwelling koalas. Rabbits were introduced to Australia and are now a major pest.

Below: Australia has an important fruit-canning industry ranging from pears and peaches to tropical fruits such as pineapples which grow in north-eastern Queensland.

New Zealand

New Zealand lies about 2000 km south-east of Australia in the Pacific Ocean. It has two main islands. North Island is where most of the people live, but South Island is larger.

New Zealand is a mountainous country. The Southern Alps run almost the full length of South Island, while in North Island there are active volcanoes, geysers and hot springs. In the high valleys of the Southern Alps are glaciers.

Few of New Zealand's swift-flowing rivers are used to carry goods, but their waters produce most of the country's electricity at hydroelectric plants.

Farming and Industry

New Zealand has fertile farmland. Fruit, cereals and other crops are grown, but the main wealth comes from sheep. Wool, meat, butter and other dairy produce are sold abroad.

Most New Zealanders live and work in towns. Mines produce coal, iron-ore and a little gold. The thick forests provide timber and paper, while the coastal waters are rich in fish.

KEY FACTS: NEW ZEALAND

Area: 268,676 sq km
Population: 3,146,000
Capital: Wellington
Highest mountain: Mount Cook (3764 metres)
Longest river: Waikato (425 km)
The chief products of New Zealand are wool, meat, dairy produce, cereals, fruits, timber and fish.

New Zealand is far from any large land mass. Australia, its nearest neighbour, is about 2000 km away.

miles
0   100   200
0   100   200
kilometres

North Cape
Auckland
Bay of Plenty
Lake Taupo
NORTH ISLAND
Wellington
Cook Strait

SOUTH ISLAND   PACIFIC OCEAN
Tasman Sea
SOUTHERN ALPS
Mt Cook 3764m
Christchurch
Banks Peninsula
Canterbury Bight
Lake Wakatipu
Lake Te Anau
Dunedin
Foveaux Strait
Stewart Island

MARIANAS ISLANDS
WAKE ISLAND
HAWAIIAN ISLANDS (U.S.A.)
JOHNSTO
MICRONESIA
CAROLINE ISLANDS (U.S.A.)
MARSHALL ISLANDS (U.S.A.)
LINE ISLANDS
KIRIBATI
PHOENIX ISLAND
MELANESIA
SOLOMON ISLANDS
TUVALU
TOKELAU
PAPUA NEW GUINEA
NEW HEBRIDES
SAMOA
Coral Sea
FIJI
COOK ISLANDS
TONGA
NEW CALEDONIA (FRANCE)
AUSTRALIA
KERMADEC ISLAN (NEW ZEALAND)
P O
Tasman Sea
NEW ZEALAND

The People of New Zealand

New Zealand's first people were the Maoris. Over 600 years ago they sailed from far across the Pacific in their canoes. Dutch sailors gave the country its name in the 1600s, and in the late 1700s the British sailor Captain Cook explored the islands. British settlers soon followed.

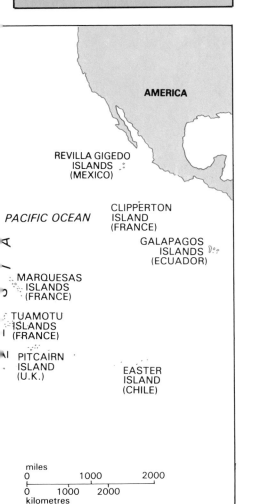

AMERICA

REVILLA GIGEDO
ISLANDS
(MEXICO)

CLIPPERTON
ISLAND
(FRANCE)

PACIFIC OCEAN

GALAPAGOS
ISLANDS
(ECUADOR)

MARQUESAS
ISLANDS
(FRANCE)

TUAMOTU
ISLANDS
(FRANCE)

PITCAIRN
ISLAND
(U.K.)

EASTER
ISLAND
(CHILE)

miles
0   1000   2000

0   1000   2000
kilometres

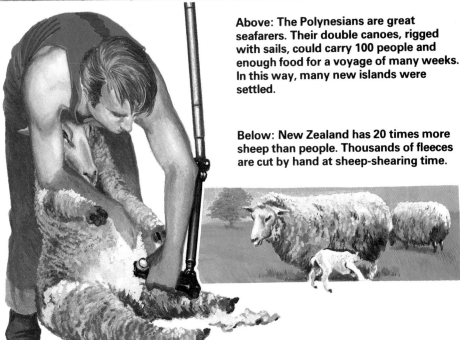

Above: The Polynesians are great seafarers. Their double canoes, rigged with sails, could carry 100 people and enough food for a voyage of many weeks. In this way, many new islands were settled.

Below: New Zealand has 20 times more sheep than people. Thousands of fleeces are cut by hand at sheep-shearing time.

The Pacific Islands

Many islands of the Pacific Ocean are part of the continent of Australasia. There are three main island groups: Micronesia, Melanesia and Polynesia.

Micronesia ('small islands') includes Nauru and Kiribati. Melanesia ('black islands') includes the Solomon Islands, Fiji and Papua New Guinea, the continent's second largest state. Polynesia ('many islands') includes Tonga, Tuvalu and Western Samoa.

The islands of Micronesia, Melanesia and Polynesia are grouped according to the people who first lived there. Micronesians have straight hair and copper coloured skins. Melanesians have dark skins and frizzy hair. Polynesians are taller than other islanders, with light brown hair. The New Zealand Maoris are Polynesians. Many islanders now live in New Zealand cities, especially Auckland.

The Poles

The Earth has two frozen zones. These are the regions around the North and South Poles – the Arctic in the north and the Antarctic in the south.

Much of the Arctic is a frozen sea called the Arctic Ocean. Around it are the snow-covered shores of North America, Europe and Asia. Farther south are the treeless plains, or tundra, where the snow melts in summer. In North America Eskimoes live by hunting and fishing. In Europe and Asia people like the Lapps herd reindeer.

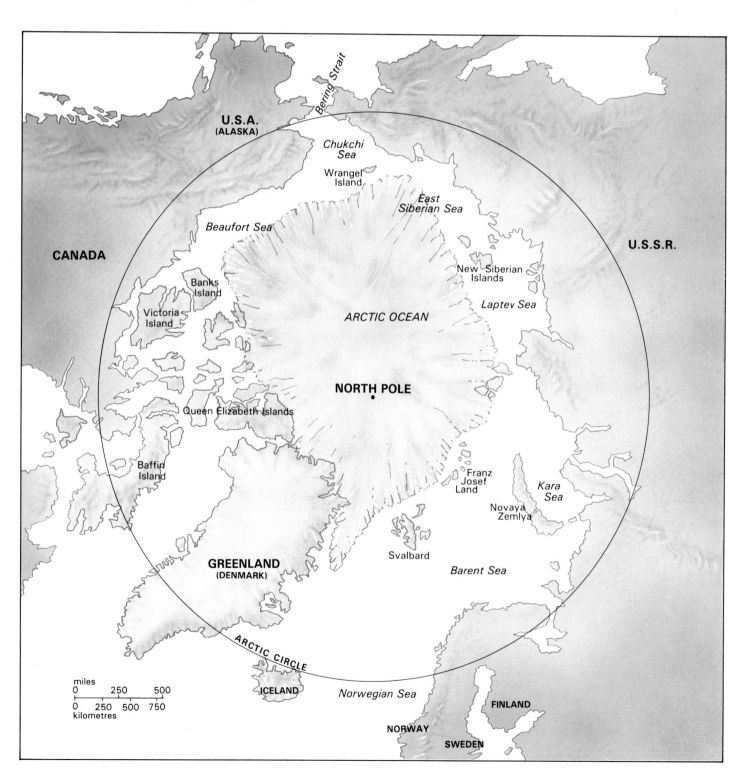

42

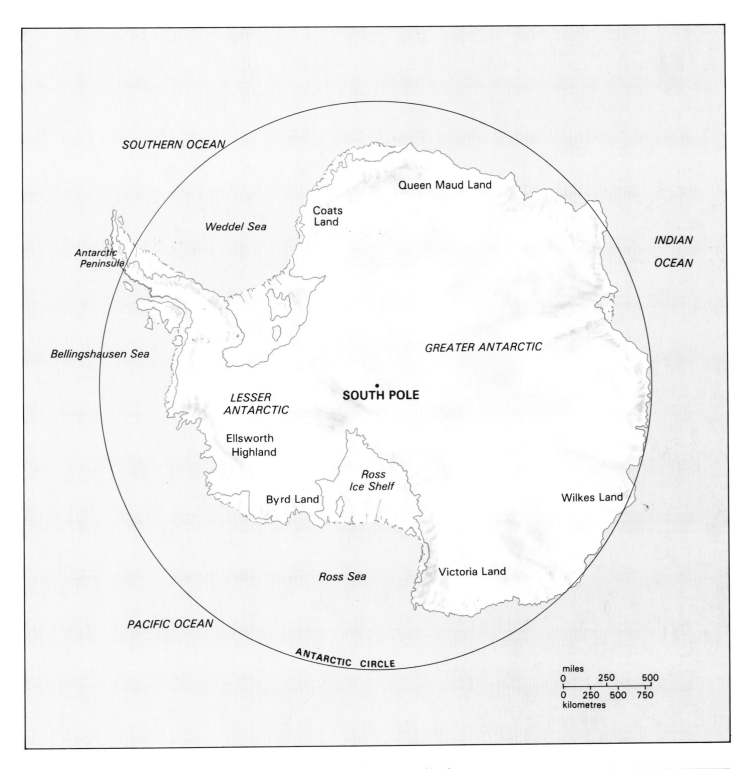

Much of the Antarctic is a frozen land continent called Antarctica. It has a rugged coast, high volcanic mountains, and a windy plain near the centre of which is the South Pole. A thick layer of ice covers the land.

The Antarctic is colder than the Arctic. It has a short summer, but the snow and ice never melt. Its only plants are a few mosses and there are no land animals. But the Antarctic Ocean is rich in plankton, fish, whales, seals and birds. The only people living in the Antarctic are scientists.

One of the things scientists have found under the ice is coal. Coal is the remains of trees which flourished in swampy forests millions of years ago. This shows that Antarctica once had a much warmer climate. Scientists believe the continent once lay nearer the equator.

KEY FACTS: THE ANTARCTIC

Area: over 14,000,000 sq km
Highest mountain: Vinson Massif (5140 metres)

The world's largest glacier is the Lambert Glacier in the Antarctic, over 60 km long.

In some places the ice is over 4500 metres thick.

The world's coldest temperature (−88.3°C) was recorded in the Antarctic in 1960.

Roald Amundsen was the first to reach the South Pole in 1911.

Index

Abidjan 24, 26
Abu Dhabi 28
Accra 24, 26
Aconcagua, Mount 15, 17
Addis Ababa 24
Adelaide 38, 39
Aden 28
Afghanistan 32
Africa 24–27
   religions of 26, 27
Alabama 13
Alaska 12, 13
Albania 20
Alberta 13
Algeria 26
Algiers 24, 26
Alps 18
Amazon River 15, 16, 17
Amman 28
Amundsen, Roald 43
Andes 15, 16
Angola 26
Ankara 28
Antananarivo 24, 26
Antarctic 43
Appalachian Mountains 10
Arctic 42
Argentina 16, 17
Arizona 13
Arkansas 13
Armenia 30
Asia 28–31
Atacama Desert 15, 16
Athens 18
Atlas Mountains 24
Auckland 40, 41
Australia 38–39
Austria 20
Ayers Rock 38, 39

Baghdad 28
Bahamas 14
Bahrain 32
Baikal, Lake 28
Balearic Islands 18
Balkan Mountains 18
Bangkok 28
Bangladesh 34, 35
Banjul 24, 26
Barbados 14
Beirut 28
Belfast 22
Belgium 20
Belgrade 18
Belize 14
Belmopan 10, 14
Benin 26
Ben Nevis 22, 23
Berbers 26
Berlin 18
Berne 18
Bhutan 34
Birmingham 22
Bissau 24, 26
Blanc, Mount 18
Blue Nile 24
Bogota 15
Bolivar, Simon 16
Bolivia 16, 17
Bonn 18
Boston 10
Botswana 26
Brahmaputra River 35, 28

Brasilia 15
Brazil 16, 17
Brisbane 38, 39
British Columbia 13
British Isles 22–23
Brussels 18
Bucharest 18
Buenos Aires 15
Bulgaria 20
Burma 34
Burundi 26
Byelorussia 30

Cairo 25
Calcutta 28
California 13
Cameroon 26
Canada 12–13
Canberra 38, 39
Cape Canaveral 12
Cape Horn 15
Cape Town 26
Caracas 15
Caribbean 14
Caroline Islands 40
Carpathian Mountains 18
Carrantuohill 22, 23
Cayenne 15
Central America 14
Chad 26
Chad, Lake 24
Cherrapunji 29
Cheviot Hills 23
Chicago 10, 13
Chile 17
China 36–37
Citlaltepetl, Mount 10
Clark, William 13
Colombia 16
Colombo 28
Colorado 13
Colorado River 11
Columbus, Christopher 11, 16
Communism, Mount 28, 31
Conakry 24, 26
Congo 26
Congo Basin 24
Connecticut 13
Cook, Captain James 39, 40
Cook, Mount 40
Copenhagen 18
Cossack 30
Costa Rica 14
Cuba 14
Czechoslovakia 20

Dacca 28
Dakar 24, 26
Damascus 28
Danube River 18
Dar-es-Salaam 24, 26
Darling River 38, 39
Darwin 38
Deccan Plain 35
Delaware 13
Delhi 28
Djibouti 24, 26
Dnieper River 30
Dominican Republic 14
Dublin 18, 22
Durban 26
Dvina River 18

Easter Island 41
Ecuador 16
Edinburgh 22
East Germany 20
EEC 20, 21
Egypt 26
Elbe River 18
Elbert, Mount 10
Elbrus, Mount 19
El Salvador 14
England 20
Erebus, Mount 43
Erie, Lake 10
Eskimo 11
Estonia 30
Ethiopia 26
Etna, Mount 18
Etosha 25
Euphrates River 28
Europe 18–21
Everest, Mount 28, 29, 34

'Fertile Crescent' 33
Fiji 40, 41
Finland 20
Florida 13
France 20
Freetown 24, 26
French Guiana 16
Fuji, Mount 37

Gabon 26
Galapagos Islands 41
Gambia River 24
Ganges River 28, 35
Gauchos 17
Georgetown 15
Georgia 13, 30
Ghana 26
Gobi Desert 28, 29, 36
Grampian Mountains 22
Grand Canyon 10, 11
Great Artesian Basin 38, 39
Great Barrier Reef 38
Great Plains 10
Great Rift Valley 25
Great Salt Lake 10
Greece 20
Guadaloupe 14
Guatemala 14
Guatemala City 10, 14
Guinea 26
Gulf of Mexico 10, 11
Guyana 16

Hague 18
Haiti 14
Hanoi 28
Harare 24, 26
Havana 10, 14
Hawaii 12
Hawaiian Islands 40
Helsinki 18
Honduras 14
Hong Kong 29
Hudson Bay 10, 11
Hudson River 11
Hungary 20
Huron, Lake 10
Hwang Ho River 36

Iceland 20
Idaho 13
Illinois 13
Incas 16
Indian Sub-Continent 34–35
Indonesia 35
Indus River 28, 34, 35
Iowa 13
Iran 32
Iraq 32
Ireland 20
Irrawaddy River 34
Israel 32
Italy 20
Ivory Coast 26

Jakarta 28
Jamaica 14
Japan 37
Jaya, Mount 34
Jerusalem 32, 33
Jordan 32

K2, Mount 28
Kabul 28
Kalahari Desert 24, 25
Kampala 24, 26
Kampuchea 34
Kansas 13
Kara Kum Desert 30
Katmandu 28
Kazakhastan 31
Kenya 26
Kenya, Mount 24, 25
Khartoum 24, 26
Kiev 30
Kilimanjaro, Mount 24, 25
Kingston 10, 14
Kinshasa 24, 26
Kiribati 40, 41
Kosciusko, Mount 39
Kuala Lumpur 28
Kuwait 32

Ladoga, Lake 18
Lagos 24, 26
Lambert Glacier 43
Laos 34
La Paz 15
Lebanon 32
Lena River 28
Lesotho 26
Lhasa 36
Liberia 26
Libreville 24, 26
Libya 26
Lilongwe 26
Lima 15
Limpopo River 24
Lisbon 18
Lithuania 30
Logan, Mount 13
Lome 24, 26
Lomond, Loch 22
London 18, 22
Londonderry 22
Los Angeles 10
Louisiana 13
Luanda 24, 26
Lusaka 24, 26
Luxembourg 18

Macchu Picchu 16
Mackenzie River 10, 13
Madeira River 15
Madrid 18
Maine 13
Malabo 24, 26
Malawi 26
Mali 26
Man, Isle of 22
Managua 10, 14
Manila 29, 35
Manitoba 13
Maoris 40
Mao Tse-tung 36
Maputo 24, 26
Maracaibo, Lake 17
Maranon River 15
Marquesas Islands 41
Martinique 14
Maryland 13
Massachusetts 13
Mauritania 26
Mbabane 24, 26
McKinley, Mount 10, 12
Mecca 32, 33
Mekong River 28, 34
Melanesia 40, 41
Malaysia 34
Melbourne 38, 39
Mexico 14
Mexico City 10, 14
Michigan 13
Michigan, Lake 10
Micronesia 40, 41
Middle East 32–33
   religions of the 33
Minnesota 13
Mississippi 13
Mississippi River 10, 11, 12
Missouri 13
Missouri River 10, 11
Moldavia 30
Mongolia 31
Monrovia 24, 26
Montana 13
Monterrey 13
Montevideo 15
Montreal 12
Morocco 26
Moscow 18, 28, 31
Mozambique 26
Murray River 38, 39
Muscat 28

N'Djamena 24, 26
Nairobi 24
Namib Desert 25
Namibia 26
Nassau 10, 14
Neagh, Lough 22
Nebraska 13
Negro River 15
Nepal 34
Netherlands 20
Ness, Loch 22
Nevada 13
New Brunswick 13
Newfoundland 13
New Hampshire 13
New Jersey 13
New Mexico 13
New Orleans 13
New York 10, 13
New Zealand 40
Niagara Falls 11
Nicaragua 14
Nicosia 28
Niger 26
Nigeria 26

Niger River 25
Nile River 24, 25
North America 11–13
North Carolina 13
North Dakota 13
North Korea 36
North Pole 42
North West Territories 13
Norway 20
Nova Scotia 13
Nyasa, Lake 24

Ob River 28, 29, 31
Oil 33
Oklahoma 13
Olympus, Mount 18
Oman 32
Onega, Lake 18
Ontario 13
Ontario, Lake 10
Orange River 24
Oregon 13
Orinoco River 15
Orkney Islands 22
Oslo 18
Ottawa 12, 13
Ouagadougou 24, 26
Oxford 22

Pacific Islands 41
Pakistan 34, 35
Pampas 15
Panama 10, 14
Panama Canal 14
Panama City 14
Pan-American Highway 14
Papua New Guinea 40, 41
Paraguay 16
Paraguay River 15
Paramaribo 15
Paris 18
Peary, Robert 42
Peking 36, 37
Pennines 22
Pennsylvania 13
Peru 16, 17
Philippines 35
Phnom Penh 28
Pico Duarte 10
Pitcairn Island 41
Plata-Parana River 16
Plymouth 22
Poland 20
Polynesia 40, 41
Poopo, Lake 15
Port au Prince 10, 14
Port Moresby 38
Porto-Novo 24, 26
Portugal 20
Prague 18
Pretoria 24, 26
Puerto Rico 14
Purus River 15
Pyrenees 18

Qatar 32
Quebec 10, 13
Quito 15

Rabat 24, 26
Rangoon 28
Reykjavik 18
Rhine River 20
Rhode Island 13
Rhone River 18
Rio de Janeiro 15, 17

Rio Grande River 10
Riyadh 28
Rocky Mountains 10, 11
Rome 18
Rumania 20
Russia 20
Rwanda 26

Sahara 24, 25
St Lawrence River 10
Salado River 15
Salto Angel 17
Salween River 34
Samoa 40, 41
San Francisco 13
San Jose 10, 14
San Juan 10, 14
San Salvador 10, 14
Santiago 15
Sao Paulo 17
Saskatchewan 13
Saudi Arabia 32
Scandinavia 18
Scotland 20
Seattle 13
Seine River 18
Selvas 15
Senegal 26
Senegal River 24
Seoul 29
Severn River 22, 23
Shanghai 29
Shannon River 22, 23
Shetland Islands 22
Shinano River 37
Siberia 28, 29, 30
Sierra Leone 26
Sierra Madre 10, 11
Singapore 34
Snowden, Mount 22
Sofia 18
Solomon Islands 40, 41
Somali Republic 26
South Africa 26
South America 15–17
South Carolina 13
South Dakota 13
South-East Asia 34–35
South Korea 37
South Pole 42, 43
South Yemen 32
Spain 20
Stockholm 18
Sudan 26
Suez Canal 24
Superior, Lake 10, 11
Surinam 16
Swansea 22
Swaziland 26
Sweden 20
Switzerland 20
Sydney 38, 39
Syria 32

Tagus River 18
Tahiti 41
Taipei 29
Taiwan 36
Tanganika, Lake 24
Tanzania 26
Taupo, Lake 40
Tegucigalpa 10, 14
Tehran 28
Tennessee 13
Texas 13
Thailand 34
Thames River 22, 23
Tierra del Fuego 15

Tigris River 28
Tirane 18
Titicaca, Lake 15, 17
Tobago 14
Togo 26
Tonga 40, 41
Toronto 13
Trent River 22
Trinidad 14
Tripoli 24, 26
Tunis 24, 28
Tunisia 26
Turkey 32
Turkmenistan 30
Tuvalu 40, 41

Uganda 26
Ukraine 30
Ulan Bator 28, 31
United Arab Emirates 32
Upper Volta 26
Ural Mountains 19
Uruguay 17
Uruguay River 15
USSR 28, 30
Utah 13

Vancouver Island 10
Vanern, Lake 18
Venezuela 16, 17
Vermont 13
Victoria, Lake 24, 25
Vienna 18
Vietnam 34
Vinson Massif 43
Virginia 13
Vistula River 18
Volga River 19, 28, 30
Vosges 18

Waikato, River 40
Wakatipu, Lake 40
Walvis Bay (South Africa) 26
Warsaw 18
Washington D.C. 10, 13
Wellington 40
West Indies 10
West Virginia 13
White Nile 24
Whitney, Mount 10
Windhoek 24, 26
Wisconsin 13
Wyoming 13

Yangtze River 29, 36, 37
Yemen 32
Yenisey River 28, 29, 30
Yugoslavia 20
Yukon 13
Yukon River 10

Zaire 26
Zaire River 24, 25
Zimbabwe 26
Zambezi River 25
Zambia 26

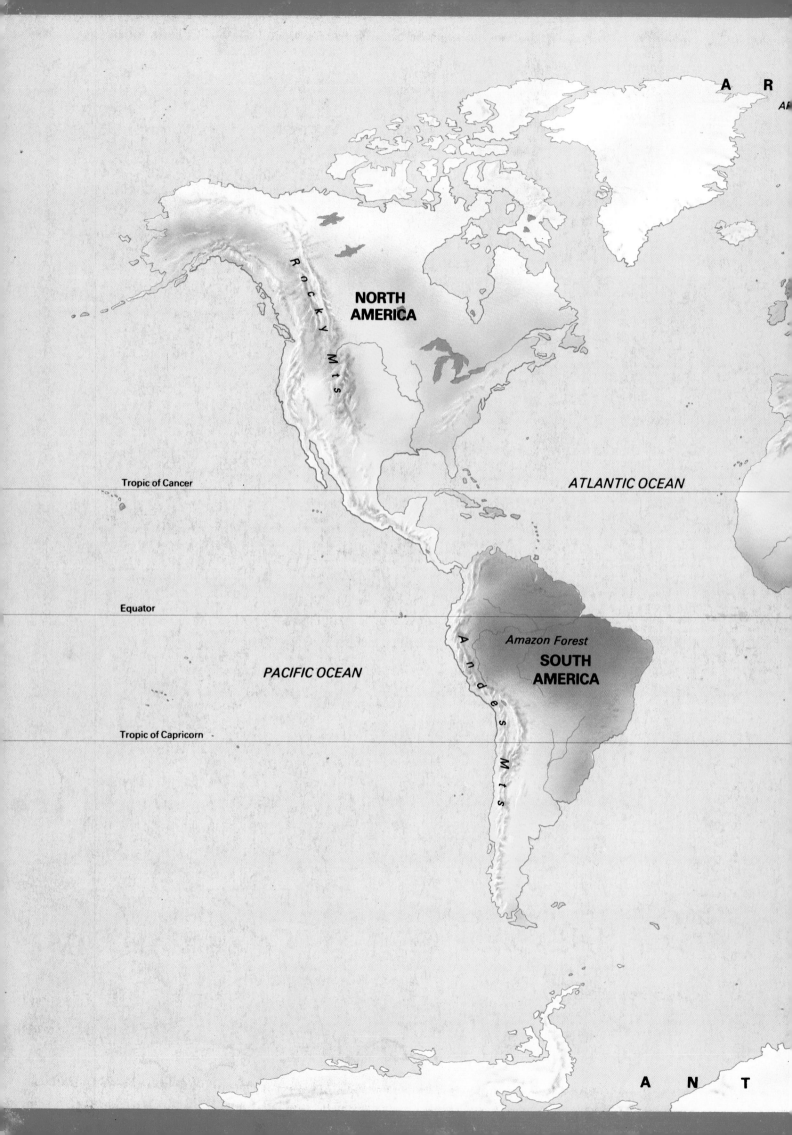

NORTH
AMERICA

Rocky Mts

ATLANTIC OCEAN

Tropic of Cancer

Equator

PACIFIC OCEAN

Amazon Forest

SOUTH
AMERICA

Andes Mts

Tropic of Capricorn

A R

A N T